SQUIRTS AND SNAILS AND SKINNY GREEN TAILS

Seashore Nature Activities for Kids

SQUIRTS AND SNAILS AND SKINNY GREEN TAILS

Seashore Nature Activities for Kids

DIANE SWANSON

Illustrations by Warren Clark

Whitecap Books

Vancouver/Toronto

Edited by Elaine Jones
Cover and interior design by Warren Clark
Cover and interior illustrations by Warren Clark
Typeset by Warren Clark

Printed and bound in Canada by D.W. Friesen and Sons Ltd.,
Altona, Manitoba

Canadian Cataloguing in Publication Data

Swanson, Diane, 1944-
    Squirts and snails and skinny green tails

    Includes bibliographical references and index.
    ISBN 1-55110-062-2

    1. Seashore biology — Juvenile literature.
I. Title.
QH95.7.S92 1993   j574.5′2638 C93-091079-6

The publisher acknowledges the assistance of the
Canada Council and the Cultural Services Branch of
the government of British Columbia in making this
publication possible.

Acknowledgments

A great many thanks go to Yousuf Ebrahim of the Biology Department, University of Victoria, for acting as my scientific advisor and reviewing the manuscript; to illustrator Warren Clark for bringing the manuscript to life with his fun and functional drawings; and to my family—Wayne, Timothy and Carolyn—for combing the seashore with me and sharing the delight that it offers.

Contents

SEASHORE ACTIVITIES

A Wood Borer Would Bore Wood	14
Rock on the Roll	18
Have a Crabby Day!	22
Pop Goes the Seaweed	27
Something Fishy	30
Eating Like a Bird	34
Happy as a Clam	39
Pools for the Stars	43
On the Moon Snail Trail	48
Hide-and-Seek—You're "It"	51
Wavy Water, Sandy Shores	56
Treasure Hunt	60

Index	64

To Kids	8
To Parents	8

SEASHORE PLANS

Where to Go	10
When to Go	10
What to Take	11

To Kids

The seashore is an amazing place. It's where pop weeds pop and sea squirts squirt...where moon snails drill and sandhoppers tunnel...where crabs walk sideways and barnacles kick food into their mouths. It's a place for discovery—a place for fun.

But before you head off, glance through this book. Read the tips on where and when to go to the seashore, and what to take with you. You may want to make the seascope on page 13. It will help you watch what goes on underwater.

At the end of your trip, plan to take the seashore home—in stories, drawings, photographs and memories. But don't plan to take home the things you find. They each play a part in seashore life. What may seem to be "only a seaweed," for instance, may be food, shelter or even a nursery for animals, like fish.

Also, please be careful when you are near water, and stay in sight of your parents.

To Parents

The ever-changing seashore is a perfect place for children to indulge their curiosity. That's why this book was written. It leads children through activities that help them discover the wonders of nature—while just having fun.

Although it's important to watch children whenever they play near water, it's not necessary to help them do the activities in this book. They can follow the simple, step-by-step instructions quite independently.

Seashore tidepools are especially

fascinating places. A section of this book invites children to observe the life in them; however, it does not encourage children to touch anything. Some plants and animals are very sensitive to handling and, on certain shores in North America, some of the tidepool life can even harm the handler. Encourage your children to discover, enjoy—and respect—the life they find.

A section called "What to Take" lists the tools children need for these activities—an inexpensive magnifying glass and a few common household items. Two other short sections, "Where to Go" and "When to Go," will help you and your children plan your seashore visits.

Whether you have time to give your children a full day or just an hour at the seashore, your gift is invaluable—for children have the ability "to see a world in a grain of sand."

Water Safety

Always keep children in sight— especially when they are wading in the water, playing along the shore's edge or kneeling beside tidepools. Be aware of incoming tides and keep well ahead of the rising water. And always, always be watchful for high waves.

Where to go

Some seashores are mainly sand or mud or rock. Some are a mixture—sandy for a stretch, then muddy or rocky. You can do some activities in this book on almost any seashore in Canada and the United States. But you will need a sandy shore for certain activities and a rocky shore for others. If you want to try many different activities in the same day, visit shores that are a mixture.

Enjoy using this book at your favorite seashore, but try exploring others, too. No two seashores are the same.

When to go

The sea responds to the pull of the moon and the sun. The water level rises, covering the shore, then it falls, uncovering plants and animals that live there. The rise and fall of the sea is called a tide. The best time to visit the seashore is when the water is low—at low tide.

How far the water rises and falls changes. But it's easy to find out when low tide occurs on a certain day. Just ask a parent to help you look it up in a tide table—a chart of water levels and times—in local newspapers.

Summer is a great season to visit the seashore, but it's also fun to go at other times of the year. And don't always wait for sunshine. If you're dressed for the weather, exploring the seashore in the rain can be just as exciting.

What to take

Clothing and Stuff

- Set of clothing you can wear in layers, like a T-shirt, a sweatshirt, a sweater and a jacket (you can change with the temperature by wearing one or more of these at a time)
- Sun hat
- Sunscreen
- Waterproof clothing, like a rainproof jacket or cape with a rainproof hat or hood (even if there is no rain, a windy day at the seashore can mean lots of spray)
- Rubber boots for wading (nice to have, but not necessary)

- Towel
- Sneakers to protect your feet from sharp objects and prevent falls on slippery rocks (take sneakers that you can get wet)
- Extra socks

Books

- This book
- Guide to life on local seashores (nice to have, but not necessary)
- Guide to life on the west and east coasts of Canada and the United States (nice to have, but not necessary). Here are two examples:

- *Seashores: A Guide to Animals and Plants along the Beaches* by Herbert Zim and Lester Ingle. New York: Golden Press, 1989.
- *An Instant Guide to Seashore Life* by Cecilia Fitzsimons. New York: Bonanza Books, 1989.

Tools for Activities

- Magnifying glass
- Small shovel or trowel
- Plastic ice cream bucket or sand pail
- Notebook (see "How to Keep a Seashore Journal")
- Pencil

- Umbrella (take it on sunny days as well as rainy ones)
- Seascope (see "How to Make a Seascope")
- Binoculars (nice to have, but not necessary)

How to Keep a Seashore Journal

It's fun to keep track of the things you see and do at seashores. That way you can remember them better—and compare them easily with what you see and do on other seashore visits.

Use a plain notebook to set up a simple seashore journal. Write the date at the top of the page. Beneath that, write the name of the seashore (if it doesn't have a name, give it one). Then write a few words about the weather. For example, you might write "hot and sunny but windy."

You can use your journal with the activities in this book. You can also use it to make lots of drawings or to jot down notes or questions about all the things you see.

How to Make a Seascope

Sometimes water is like a mirror. When you look into it, you mostly see yourself. A seascope can help you see into the water more clearly. And it is easy and fast to make.

What You Need

- 2-liter or half-gallon milk carton

- Scissors
- Plastic food wrap, sold under various names
- Transparent tape
- Two elastic bands

What to Do

1. Cut off the top and bottom of the milk carton.
2. Tear off a piece of plastic food wrap about 50 centimeters (20 inches) long.

3. Stand the carton in the middle of the wrap.
4. Fold up the wrap on all sides of the carton and tape the ends to the carton.

5. Put two elastic bands around the plastic wrap and the carton: one near the top and one near the bottom.
6. Use your seascope by putting the plastic-covered end into the water and the open end close to your face.

A Wood Borer Would Bore Wood

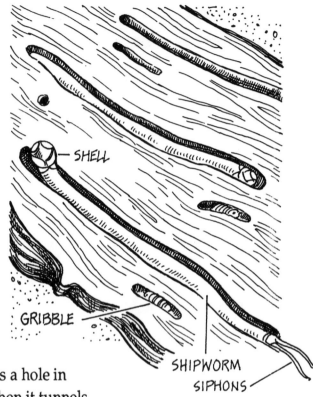

When is a worm really a clam that is called a termite? When it's a shipworm—a clam with two small shells attached to a long, wormlike body. Shipworms bore wood—like termites do. And so do gribbles, which are tiny, 14-legged sea animals. Shipworms and gribbles are wood borers that can turn a boat or wharf into sawdust. That's why people call them "termites of the sea."

Scraping with its shells, a shipworm bores a hole in wood and cements its end to the opening. Then it tunnels through the wood as it grows. Its shells are not even as wide as your little fingernail, but its body usually grows to about ruler length—30 centimeters (12 inches). A shipworm puts out tubes called siphons to pump water in and out. It lives on the oxygen and bits of food in the water.

The gribble, which is only about as big as the letter "O," uses its mouth to bore wood. It feeds on fungus—plantlike material—that grows in the wood, as well as a bit of the wood itself.

GRIBBLE

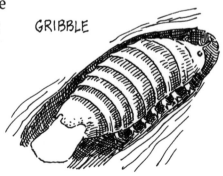

Discover Driftwood

1. Search high along the shore for logs, planks and other driftwood thrown by waves or left by tides.

2. Check the color. Wood that has just been washed up will likely be brown or reddish. Wood that has been lying on the shore for a few weeks looks gray. No matter what color it once was, sea weather soon turns all wood the same dull shade. Try scraping gray driftwood with your trowel to see what color is underneath.

3. Feel the ends of large and small pieces of driftwood. They likely are smooth and rounded—worn by the water.

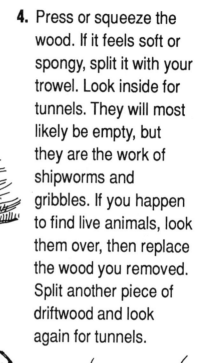

4. Press or squeeze the wood. If it feels soft or spongy, split it with your trowel. Look inside for tunnels. They will most likely be empty, but they are the work of shipworms and gribbles. If you happen to find live animals, look them over, then replace the wood you removed. Split another piece of driftwood and look again for tunnels.

Sort Tunnels

1. Check out the tunnels in the driftwood that you split. Shipworm tunnels are long, but gribble tunnels are shorter than a paper clip.

2. Check the width of the tunnels. If you can slide a pencil through one, a shipworm probably made it. Gribbles make much narrower tunnels.

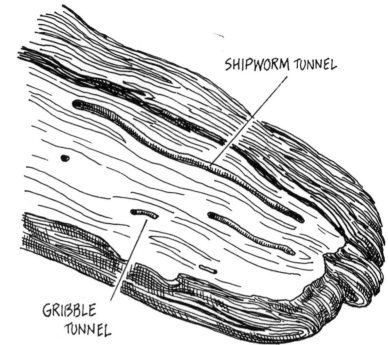

SHIPWORM TUNNEL

GRIBBLE TUNNEL

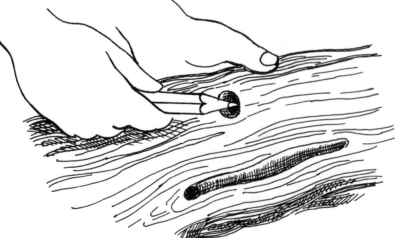

3. Check the tunnel walls. Shipworms line them with a thin, chalky material. Gribbles don't line their tunnels at all. Instead, if a roof begins to flake, a gribble usually bores a new tunnel.

Scribbles on Gribbles...and More

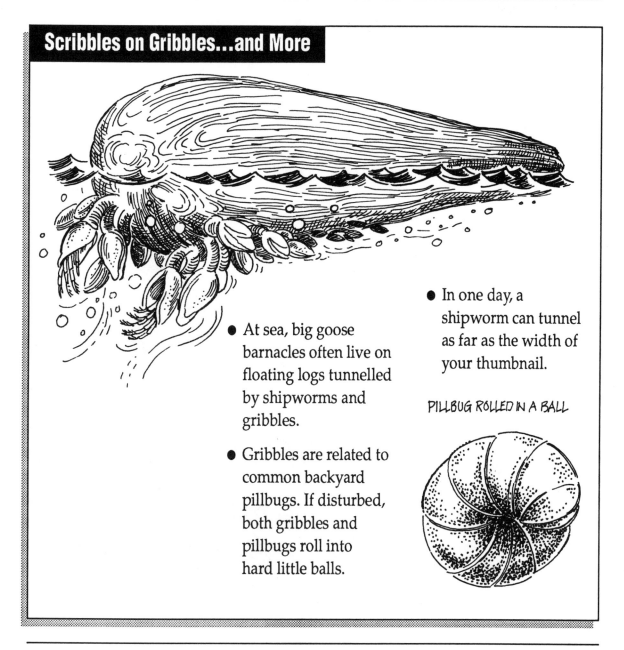

- At sea, big goose barnacles often live on floating logs tunnelled by shipworms and gribbles.

- Gribbles are related to common backyard pillbugs. If disturbed, both gribbles and pillbugs roll into hard little balls.

- In one day, a shipworm can tunnel as far as the width of your thumbnail.

PILLBUG ROLLED IN A BALL

Rock on the Roll

Year after year, the sea hammers the shores. It pounds air and water into cracks in rocks and cliffs. Bit by bit, the cracks open, then chunks of rock fall into the sea.

Waves use these chunks to pound the shore—and other chunks of rock. Over time, the wave-tossed rock gets smaller and smaller, gradually becoming little pebbles and tiny grains of sand.

Sand and pebbles get their color from the rocks they once were. But shores are made from mixtures of rocks. Many sandy shores, for instance, have billions of gray and white grains of a hard mineral called quartz. But they usually also have sand that is brown, red and black— from other rocks. Sea pebbles are often red, gold, green, white and black.

See, Hear and Feel the Pebbles

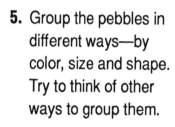

1. Kneel near the edge of the seashore where you can see some pebbles under water. Watch them closely as waves wash in. Notice how the pebbles move.

2. Put your ear close to the water and listen. You may hear the pebbles clicking against each other as they tumble.

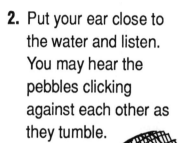

3. Scoop up a handful of pebbles. Feel how rounded the pebbles are. They smooth each other as they tumble together.

4. Notice how shiny and colorful the pebbles look when they are wet. Then lay them some place away from the water. Check the pebbles after they have dried to see if they are still shiny and colorful.

5. Group the pebbles in different ways—by color, size and shape. Try to think of other ways to group them.

6. Place the pebbles back where you found them.

Scoop, Stamp and Soak the Sand

1. Scoop up a handful of dry sand. Use your magnifying glass to look at the tiny grains up close. Notice the different colors.

2. Check the shape of the grains of sand. Most are jagged—not smooth. Rub the sand between your fingers and notice how it feels: powdery or gritty.

3. Take off your socks and sneakers. Stamp your bare feet on dry sand, then wriggle your toes. If you can bury your feet easily, the grains are coarse. If the sand feels firm beneath your feet and toes, the grains are fine. There is more space between grains of coarse sand than between grains of fine sand.

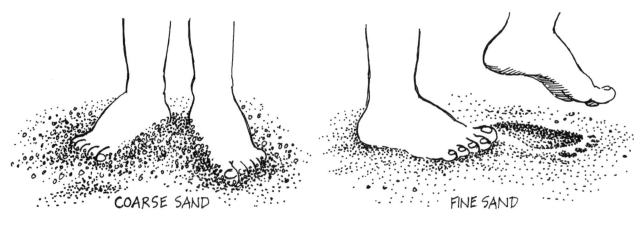

COARSE SAND

FINE SAND

4. Fill a bucket with sea water and pour it onto dry sand—well away from the sea. After the water soaks in, quickly dig with a trowel or small shovel to see how far down the water went. Water sinks more deeply in coarse sand than in fine sand.

5. Look for both kinds of sand—coarse and fine—and pour water on each. Compare what happens.

6. Remember to fill in all the holes you dig.

Rock Beat

● On some unprotected shores, powerful waves cut cliffs back 6 meters (20 feet) a year—that's about the length of three beds placed end to end.

● Builders use common quartz sand to make many things, like sidewalks, bridges and buildings.

● On one Pacific shore in the United States, the waves created a small beach—not out of pebbles or sand—but out of tin cans washed from a nearby garbage dump.

Have a Crabby Day!

C rabs scurry along rocky, sandy and muddy shores all around the world. Although they come in many colors, shapes and sizes, true crabs each have five pairs of legs: four pairs for walking and one pair, with pincers, for grabbing food and fighting.

A crab can see in every direction. That's because its eyes turn right around on two stalks on top of its head. Two pairs of feelers between its eyes allow the crab to touch and smell.

The hard shell that protects a crab's soft body never grows. Instead, it splits when it becomes too tight, and the crab slips out the back. The soft body of the crab grows fast for three or four days, then a new shell hardens around it. Many adult crabs molt— shed their shells—every year. Young crabs molt more often.

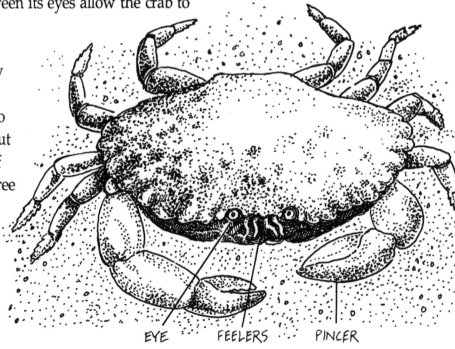

EYE   FEELERS   PINCER

Check for Crabs

1. At low tide, search for crabs in their common hiding spots.
   - Look among loose stones and gravel.
   - Peek in cracks in and between rocks.
   - Look under rocks.
   - Peer into pools of water on rocky shores.
   - Scan shallow water along the shore.
   - Check around seaweed.

2. Notice how flat a crab is. Check the color and markings on its shell. They help the crab blend with its surroundings so its enemies can't see it easily.

3. Watch for crabs of different colors and with other markings. You may have to explore different parts of the seashore.

4. Try to get close enough to see a crab's eyes and the feelers between the eyes.

5. Watch a crab walk— usually sideways. It pushes with four legs on one side of its body and pulls with four legs on the other side.

6. Put your hands on the shore. Use your two pairs of "legs" to walk sideways—pushing and pulling like a crab.

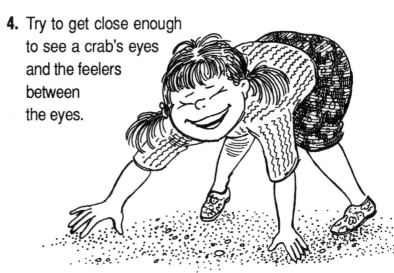

Search for Shells

1. Look for empty crab shells along the shore. Some are the remains of dead crabs, but many are shells that crabs have molted.

2. Check for a slit between the back and the "tail" of a crab shell—a sign of molting. The tail is the part of the crab that is wrapped under its body. A female crab has a much wider tail than a male crab. She uses it to carry her eggs.

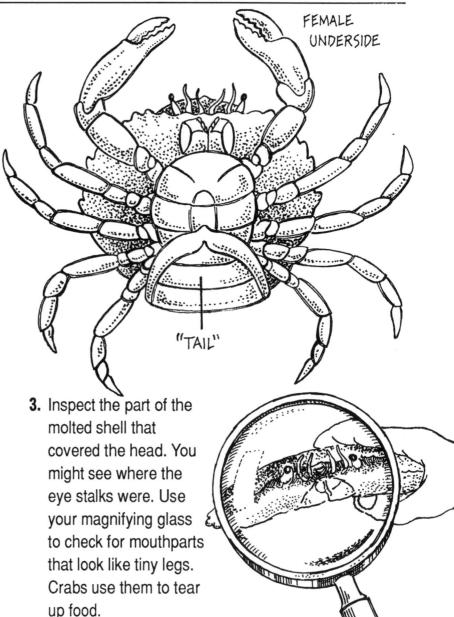

FEMALE UNDERSIDE

"TAIL"

3. Inspect the part of the molted shell that covered the head. You might see where the eye stalks were. Use your magnifying glass to check for mouthparts that look like tiny legs. Crabs use them to tear up food.

4. Put the empty crab shells you find into two groups: those with wide tails (female) and those with narrow tails (male). Count the shells in each group and write the numbers in your notebook. Compare these numbers with the numbers of male and female crab shells you find on your next visit.

5. Leave the crab shells on the shore.

Crab Gab

- Spider crabs—like spiders—have long, skinny legs. One kind of spider crab, a decorator crab, sticks seaweed, sponge and other sea life on its back so it can hide.

- The biggest crab is the Japanese spider crab that lives in deep water. Its long legs nearly span the length of two beds placed end to end.

- Pairs of tiny pea crabs commonly live inside the shells of some live clams.

Hunt for Hermits

1. At low tide, look among pebbles on the shore, in shallow water along the shore or in pools of water on rocky shores. Watch for an animal with the shell of a snail but the head and legs of a crab. That's a hermit crab, not a true crab. The hermit doesn't have its own complete shell, so it helps protect itself with empty shells from snails. As it grows, it moves into bigger shells.

2. Notice the curved shape of the shell. The soft body of the hermit crab curves to fit the shell.

3. Watch the hermit crab walk, dragging its shell along. It usually walks on just two pairs of legs. Another two pairs help the crab hold the shell on.

4. GENTLY scoop up the shell and place it on your open hand. See how fast the hermit crab tucks itself inside. It will likely use its large pincer to close off the shell's opening. Use your magnifying glass to look closely.

5. GENTLY place the shell back where it was. Wait patiently. See how long it takes before the hermit crab appears again.

6. Try to find another hermit crab. Compare the size, shape and color of its shell with the shell of the first hermit crab you saw.

Pop Goes the Seaweed

B ushy and stringy, lumpy and smooth, long and short. Thousands of kinds of seaweed live in the sea, but there are three main groups: green, brown and red.

Seaweed has no roots, or real stems or leaves. But many kinds have tough, rubbery stemlike parts, called stipes, that can bend easily in strong waves. And many have holdfasts—rootlike parts that anchor the stipes to rocks and other hard things. Some kinds of seaweed also have air sacs that act like floating balloons. These sacs hold the seaweed's blades up to the light.

Lots of animals need seaweed. For some animals, it is food. For others, it is a place to lay eggs or hide from hungry enemies, crashing waves and harsh weather. Even people use seaweed for many things, like food, fertilizer and medicine.

AIR SAC

STIPE   HOLDFAST   BLADE

Find Some Lettuce, Popping Weeds and More

1. Look for seaweed at low tide, especially along rocky shores. But avoid walking on seaweed on rocks—it's slippery. Don't look in spots where rivers meet the sea. Not much seaweed grows there.

2. Look for green seaweed on rocks and pilings in shallow water. Watch how some kinds wave or bend as the water moves. Count the different kinds you see. Notice how seaweed looks different in the air than in water.

3. Search for sea lettuce, a bright green seaweed with wide, curly blades. Draw the shape of sea lettuce in your notebook. Don't taste it, but when you get home, compare the shape with the shape of the lettuce that you eat.

4. Hunt for brown and red seaweed washed up on the shore—especially after a storm. Brown seaweed generally grows in deeper water than green seaweed. Red kinds usually grow in even deeper water. Check the ends for holdfasts. Feel how slippery the blades are. See how easily you can bend the stipes.

5. Find some rockweed, bladder wrack, popping wrack or pop weed—all names for the same brown seaweed. Most kinds have air sacs. Try popping some with your fingers and listen to the air escape. Float some rockweed along the water's edge and notice how the air sacs keep the blades up.

Seaweed Wonders

- On the west coast of North America, a brown seaweed called bull kelp can grow up to 30 meters (100 feet)—taller than some 10-story buildings.

- One kind of seaweed, called an oyster thief, attaches its holdfast to an oyster shell. At high tide, the thief floats away with its air sacs, taking the oyster, too.

- A broken part from a rockweed will keep growing and form a new plant.

Something Fishy

One of the fastest animals at the seashore is the fish. Built to swim, fish dart through the water, turning and circling with ease.

Scientists think about 30,000 different kinds of fish live on Earth, and among them, there are fish of every color. But many of the fish that swim near the surface of the sea are silver. That's so birds and other enemies can't spot them easily in bright water.

The skin of most fish is covered with scales set in little pockets. The scales get bigger as fish grow—something they never stop doing. But as they age, fish and their scales grow more slowly.

Fish always seem to be staring. That's because they have no eyelids. But although their eyes are always open, they manage to rest, usually by taking several little naps a day.

Play Rock "Music" for Fish

1. Pick up two fist-sized rocks and wade into clear, shallow water close to shore.

2. Hold the rocks underwater. Tap or scratch one rock on the other several times. Sound travels well through water. Your rock "music" may interest some fish.

3. Stand very still—like the great blue heron on page 35. Watch the water closely. If you spot some fish, don't move towards them. Stay where you are and let the fish come to you.

4. Watch as the fish move nearby. Notice how easily they swim, stop and turn.

5. If no fish appear, repeat steps 2, 3 and 4. Try this activity in other clear, shallow water along the shore. See how many fish you can attract with your rock "music."

Watch Fish on the Go

1. Look for fish—big or small—in clear, shallow water or in pools of water on rocky shores. If you made the seascope on page 13, you may want to use it here. Or you may want to hold up an umbrella to reduce glare from the water. Your shadow might make the fish hide. Be patient and don't move, and they will probably come out where you can see them.

2. Watch how most fish move—by swishing their strong tails from side to side.

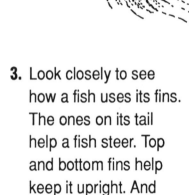

3. Look closely to see how a fish uses its fins. The ones on its tail help a fish steer. Top and bottom fins help keep it upright. And side fins act something like boat oars. The fish uses them to move forward, stop, back up and turn.

4. Notice how well a fish can hover in the water. When it stops swimming, it neither sinks nor floats to the top. That's because many kinds of fish have air sacs in their bodies. Air in these sacs helps fish stay in one spot.

Fish can also rise by increasing the air in their sacs and sink by decreasing it.

5. Watch a fish breathe. It opens its mouth and takes in water. The fish uses organs, called gills, to take oxygen from the water. Watch

GILL COVER

the gill covers move as the water comes back out.

Fantastic Fish Facts

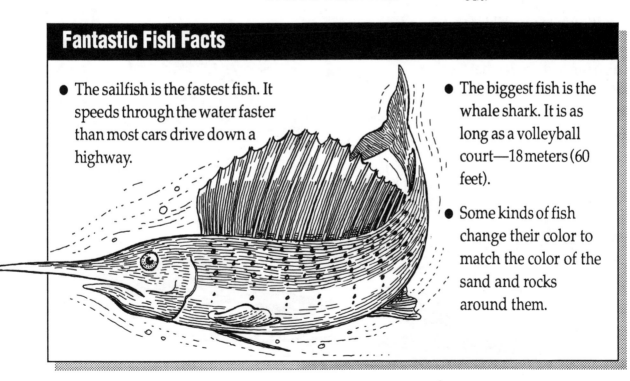

- The sailfish is the fastest fish. It speeds through the water faster than most cars drive down a highway.

- The biggest fish is the whale shark. It is as long as a volleyball court—18 meters (60 feet).

- Some kinds of fish change their color to match the color of the sand and rocks around them.

33

Eating Like a Bird

A t the seashore, birds come in all shapes and sizes. And they all come hungry. Many eat their weight in food every day—but they have to find it first.

How birds look for food depends on the kind of bird they are. Some wade in shallow water. Some swim and dive in the sea. Others do both. And you may see birds finding food in other ways as well.

It's fun to watch birds catch and eat their food at the seashore. It's also fun to discover that "eating like a bird" really means eating a lot—not a little—like many people wrongly believe.

Watch the Waders

1. Watch for birds walking along the shore's edge and wading in shallow water. Use binoculars if you can. Look for big birds and small ones. See how many different kinds you can spot. In your notebook, write down the number of waders you see. On another seashore trip, compare this number with the number of waders you count then.

2. Look at the birds' legs and feet. Waders have long legs for the size of their bodies. And they have long toes to help them walk on mud and sand. If you can't see their feet, check their footprints after the birds have gone.

3. Notice that many waders have long necks and bills. They help the birds catch fish or poke in sand and seaweed for food, such as worms and crabs. Watch the waders to see if they find food.

4. Scan the shore for a great blue heron—a common wader. It may be as tall as you— about 1 meter (3 to 4 feet), with a long, curving neck and a tuft of feathers on its head. Watch the heron patiently. It often stands as still as stone, then suddenly, it may snatch a passing fish. The heron points its beak to the sky and the fish slides down the bird's long neck.

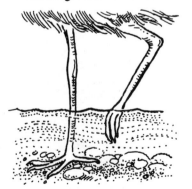

5. Watch the heron some more. It often walks very slowly, taking many minutes to lift one leg from the water and move one step. Try walking as slowly as that.

Spot the Swimmers

1. Look for birds swimming on the sea. Use binoculars if you can. Swimming birds have webbed feet or toes like paddles that help them swim.

See how many different kinds you can spot, then open your notebook. Below the number of waders, write down the number of swimmers you see. On another seashore trip, compare this number with the number of swimmers you count then.

2. See if the swimmers try to catch a meal. Some scoop for food near the water's surface. Some dive for food, such as shellfish or seaweed. Some swim well underwater, using their strong wings to help.

3. Watch these birds along the shore. You may see one use its bill to take oil from a place near its tail. Then the bird rubs the oil into its feathers to waterproof them.

4. See if you can spot some ducks—common swimmers. You may notice some swimming with their heads underwater, then diving. Or you may see a duck fly low over the water, then dive from the air. Some of these ducks have rough beaks to grasp slippery fish.

Bird Blurbs

- One kind of duck, called an oldsquaw, dives down to 60 meters (200 feet) to get food. A building more than 20 stories tall would be covered by water that deep.

- When they are hungry, young gulls peck the red spot on their parent's bill. Then the parent brings up partly digested food and feeds its young.

- A heron sometimes drops a feather from its beak, then snaps up the fish that swims to the feather.

5. Look for a cormorant, a big, black bird with a brightly colored patch on its throat. It swims, then dives—often very deep—using its long neck and hooked bill to catch fish. But its feathered coat is not waterproof. After fishing, the cormorant holds its wings out to dry. Watch for it on rocks offshore.

Gawk at Gulls

1. Look for the seashore's eating experts, the gulls. They eat almost anything—even a fat sea star, which they swallow whole. They catch their food by wading, by swimming and diving, and just by poking around.

2. Find more than one kind of gull. They are sturdy birds with long, pointed wings but their color varies. Some are brownish. Many are white, black or gray—or a mix of these colors.

3. Notice the gull's long legs for wading and its hooked bill for poking among seaweed, under rocks and in mud.

4. Try to spot a gull with a shellfish. The gull will likely fly over a rock, drop the shellfish, then check for cracks in the shell. To get at the meal inside, the gull will drop a shellfish until it cracks.

5. Watch gulls feed in the water. They are strong swimmers and they duck underwater to grab food. Their hooked bills help them catch fish.

6. Notice how gulls clean up a seashore. They eat dead animals, scraps from fishing boats and many other things.

Happy as a Clam

Lots of clams live on seashores, but you won't likely see any unless you dig. They usually bury themselves in sand, mud or gravel, sending up tubes, called siphons, to reach the water at high tides. Most have two siphons: one to draw water in and one to shoot it out. The water carries in oxygen and tiny bits of food. Some kinds of clams use their "in" siphons—like vacuum cleaners—to suck up food lying on a shore.

A clam digs down with its strong foot. The tip of the foot expands to anchor the clam so it can pull its body down. Then the foot can dig some more.

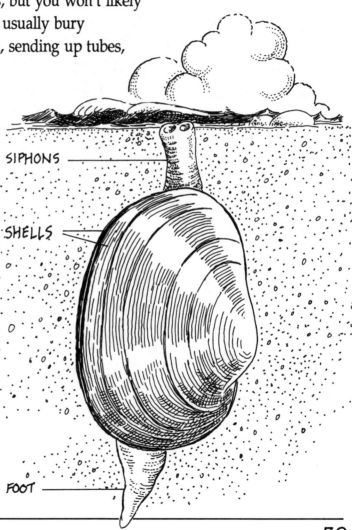

SIPHONS

SHELLS

FOOT

Race a Clam

1. At low tide, hunt for clam clues.
   - Search for small holes in mud or sand on the open shore.
   - Look under stones and boulders for holes in mud and sand.
   - Watch for water squirting out of the shore. It may squirt high on your legs.

2. Grab your trowel or shovel when you spot a clam clue. Start digging about as far from the clue as the length of your foot. That way you won't likely break the clam's shells.

3. Dig several scoops of sand or mud—and hurry. Some clams dig surprisingly fast.

4. Drop your trowel or shovel and feel quickly through the wet sand.

5. If the clam gets away, fill in your hole. Then repeat steps 1 to 4. If you find a clam, read on.

Look a Clam Over

1. Hold a live clam GENTLY. See if any of the clam's soft body, foot or siphons are sticking outside of its shells. Some kinds of clams can draw everything in and close up tightly. Others do not have room to draw all their parts inside. Their shells never close completely.

2. Notice the size, shape and color of the clam. It's just one of about 800 different kinds around the world.

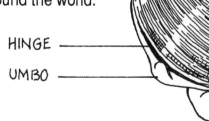

HINGE ———

UMBO ———

3. Find the oldest part of the clam's shells: the umbo. It's a bump near the hinge that joins the two shells.

4. Run your fingers over the ridges in the shells. As a clam grows, it adds more hard material to the shell's edges and builds these ridges. The more ridges there are, the older the clam is.

5. Put the clam back where you found it and fill in your hole.

6. Search for more clams. Try to find different kinds. Compare their sizes, shapes and colors.

7. Walk along the shore and look for empty clam shells.
   - Feel the undersides that once touched the clam's soft body. Notice how smooth they are.
   - Find the two scars where the clam's strong

muscles were. They closed the shells.

- Check the umbo area. If you see a neat, round hole, you've discovered a clue about how the clam might have died. To find out more, try the moon snail activities on pages 48 to 50.

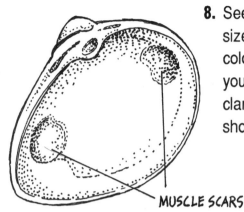

MUSCLE SCARS

8. See how many different sizes, shapes and colors of clam shells you can find. Leave the clam shells on the shore.

Clam Whammies

- The razor clam is a speedy digger. In 60 seconds, it can burrow more than two ruler lengths— 60 centimeters (24 inches).

- The slowest-growing animal is likely the deep-sea clam of the Atlantic Ocean. It takes about 100 years to grow to be as long as the width of your little fingernail.

- The piddock clam of North America bores into rock or concrete. It stays there for life.

Pools for the Stars

When tides fall, they leave pools of water in pits and hollows along rocky shores. Each of these tidepools is a natural aquarium, filled with hundreds of different kinds of plants and animals. When tides rise, the sea covers the pools again.

Life in tidepools carries on much like it does in the sea, so pools give people a chance to see what happens underwater. And the sights are great: purple sea stars creeping across rocks, fish darting in and out of shadows, and flowerlike sea anemones trapping tiny crabs.

Peek in a Pool

1. Check the tidepools along a rocky shore CAREFULLY: the rocks around them are usually slippery. Find a pool that is quite shallow but has lots of life in it.

2. Count the different kinds of life you see in the pool. Don't forget to look into cracks and under ledges. With a stick or pencil, wiggle seaweed GENTLY. A little fish, crab or some other animal might appear.

3. If the day is very sunny, reduce glare from the water so you can see better. Hold up an umbrella to make shade or bring out your seascope if you made one (see page 13). If you have a small magnifying glass, lay it on the inside bottom of your seascope. Before putting your seascope into the water, be sure to kneel on a steady rock, and remember not to lean too far out.

4. Try to stay as still as you can so you can watch the animals in the tidepool. Your shadow may cause them to hide or stay very still at first. But if you don't move, life in the tidepool will soon carry on.

5. Notice which animals move and how fast—or slow—they go. You might be lucky enough to see an animal feed.

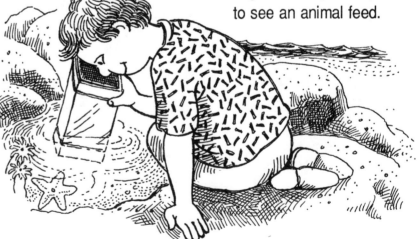

Cool Pool Creatures

- Two of the oddest places barnacles live are a whale's nose and a penguin's toes.

- A whole new sea star can grow from one arm and a bit of its center disk.

- Sea urchins are covered with so many sharp spines that people call them "porcupines of the sea." But when the urchins die, these spines all fall off.

6. Watch for some of the common tidepool animals in the chart. Make a list of the ones you spot. Compare what you see in different tidepools and on different days. Each pool is special and always changing.

7. Compare the sea anemones, barnacles and mussels you see in tidepools (see the chart) with the ones you see in drier places. Notice when they look open and when they look closed.

REMEMBER:
Touching some animals in tidepools on some shores can harm you—and them. It's best just to peek in. That way you can see how the animals really live.

Ten Common Tidepool Animals

Sea star

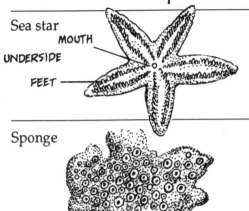

MOUTH

UNDERSIDE

FEET

- Moves slowly in any direction using hundreds of suction-tipped feet in rows under its arms.
- Uses its feet to open a shellfish just a crack, then pokes its stomach—inside out—through its mouth and into the shellfish to feed.

Sponge

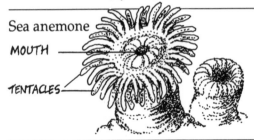

- Stays attached to rocks or shells (some sponges look like splashes of pink or orange paint).
- Uses many holes in its soft body to take in water holding plants and animals so small you can't see them.

Sea anemone

MOUTH

TENTACLES

- Usually stays attached to shells or rocks, but can move very slowly (some anemones look like green or purple flowers).
- Uses tentacles around its mouth to sting and trap animals—like shrimp and crabs—but tucks the tentacles inside when in danger or dry air.

Barnacle

FEET

- Stays attached to shells, rocks and other smooth objects.
- Sticks its feathery feet out of its shell to kick plant and animal bits from the water into its mouth, but closes its shell in dry air.

Mussel

- Usually stays attached to rocks, pilings and other mussels.
- Opens its shells slightly and strains plant and animal bits out of the water, but closes its shells in dry air.

Limpet
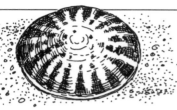

- Usually stays still during the daytime, but at night it glides slowly on one long foot, hunting for food.
- Uses a tongue lined with teeth to scrape plants off rocks.

Chiton
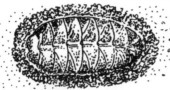

- Moves like the limpet (above).
- Feeds like the limpet (above).

Sea urchin SKELETON
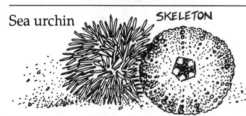

- Moves slowly on rows of little tube feet and sharp spines, which also protect it.
- Uses five teeth in its mouth underneath to scrape and chew food, such as seaweed. (Compare with a skeleton you find on the shore.)

Fish

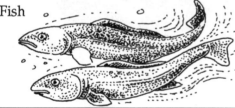

- Usually swims quickly by moving its tail from side to side.
- Eats bits of plants and animals in the water or catches small animals, such as shrimp. (See fish activities on pages 30 to 33.)

Crab

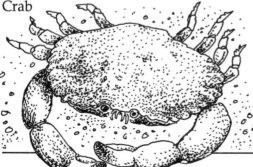

- Usually moves quite fast on eight legs— sideways.
- Eats dead animals and catches little fish, worms, shellfish and other small animals. Some kinds of crabs eat seaweed. (See crab activities on pages 22 to 26.)

On the Moon Snail Trail

On many gentle sandy shores lives the beautiful moon snail. Like land snails, it has only one shell. But what a shell it is: wide, curled and up to 14 centimeters (5.5 inches) high—about half a ruler length. Depending on the kind of moon snail, the shell may be creamy white, gray, tan, silver or pink.

But the moon snail is more than just a pretty shell. It is a skilled hunter. With acid from the tip of its tongue, the snail can soften the hard shell of an animal, like a clam. Then, with the teeth on its tongue, the moon snail drills a hole right through the shell. The long tongue digs out the clam's soft body so the moon snail can feed.

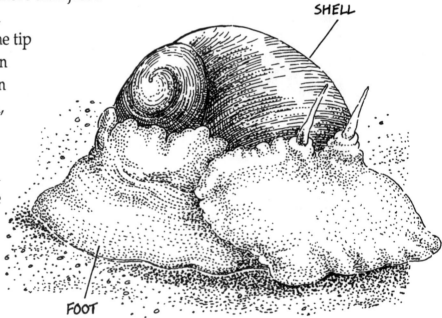

SHELL

FOOT

Unveil a Snail

1. Wade in clear, shallow water along the edge of a sandy shore at low tide. If you made the seascope on page 13, you may want to use it here. Watch for a little, slow-moving mound of sand. Moon snails spend most of their time beneath the sand, hunting for food.

2. GENTLY swish away the sand. You will likely uncover a moon snail. Take a close look.

3. Notice the moon snail's big, fleshy foot all around its shell. The moon snail uses this foot to get around—gliding in or on the sand. A fold of the foot, like a hood, protects its eyes from the sand. Sometimes, the foot smothers the moon snail's prey or holds the animal while the moon snail drills through its shell.

4. Feel in the sand just ahead of the snail. You may find what the snail is after—a clam, perhaps. Small moon snails eat clams that can't pull all of themselves into their shells. But large moon snails can drill and eat clams that close up tightly.

Hold the Moon in Your Hands

1. GENTLY scoop up the moon snail and lay it across your hands. Notice how slippery it is. Feel its slimy foot. Because you have disturbed the moon snail, it will likely pull itself into its shell.

2. Watch how the snail fits its big foot inside. It has to squeeze out lots of water to do that.

3. Check to see how the moon snail closes off its shell after it pulls itself inside. Look with your magnifying glass.

4. GENTLY place the moon snail back where you found it. Watch to see if the foot reappears and takes the snail off again.

Marvellous Moon Snails

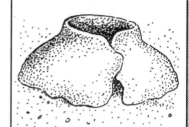

- A moon snail uses mucus and sand to stick thousands of its tiny eggs together in a ring. When the ring crumbles, young moon snails hatch.

- Some kinds of moon snails eat six or seven clams in a day.

- When the teeth on its tongue wear down, the moon snail grows new ones.

Hide-and-Seek — You're "It"

I magine arriving at a seashore and finding it empty. As far as you can see, nothing is moving. That happens sometimes. But it doesn't mean that all the animals have left the shore. They just may be hiding.

Animals have good reasons for hiding. They want to avoid being eaten. Sometimes they hide so they can catch other animals by surprise. They also hide to protect themselves from pounding waves, burning sunshine, drying winds and freezing temperatures.

Dig the Seashore

1. Pick a spot anywhere on a sandy or muddy shore and dig. Small animals, like insects and worms, live in the sand and mud. See what you can uncover. Use your magnifying glass to look closely. Remember to fill in the holes that you dig.

2. Try to find a lugworm. Crawl along the shore, watching for little coiled mounds of sand or mud. Each of these mounds marks one end of a lugworm's U-shaped burrow. Finding a mound is not as hard as it sounds. On some seashores, there may be thousands.

3. Dig GENTLY with your trowel or shovel close to the mound. You will likely uncover a greenish or brownish lugworm. It sucks in sand or mud that contains bits of food, then expels the sand and mud. The lugworm pushes it all out of the burrow—as a little coiled mound.

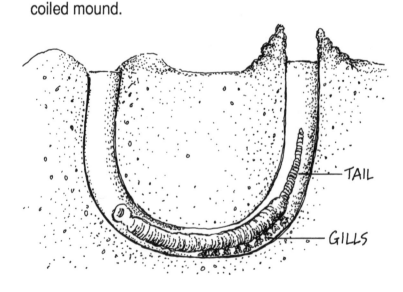

TAIL

GILLS

4. GENTLY hold the lugworm or lay it on your trowel or shovel. Notice its feathery red "bristles." They are gills, used for breathing. Find the lugworm's tail—the skinniest part of its body.

5. Free the lugworm and watch to see how quickly it works its way back into the shore. Fill in the hole you dug.

Seashore Secrets

● In just five minutes, a sandhopper can dig a hole deeper than three sandhoppers end to end. That's like you digging a hole deeper than three of your friends in five minutes—without a shovel.

● The sea squirt's heart pumps blood through its body—sending it first one direction, then the other direction.

Check the Garbage

1. Walk high along the shore to see the garbage that waves have washed in: torn seaweed, empty shells, bones, driftwood, dead animals, and even human garbage, like tins, rope and plastic bottles.

2. Lift some of the garbage and dig in the sand around it. See what's hiding underneath. Look for a sandhopper, a high-jumping animal less than half as long as your little finger. It's also called a beach hopper or a beach flea. Garbage is one of the things it eats.

3. Watch how well a sandhopper jumps— like a flea—but the sandhopper is not an insect. It is related to shrimp and barnacles. Now watch to see if any sandhoppers tunnel back into the sand or dig under the garbage where they spend their days. At night, lots of them hop about on the shore.

Explore the Rocks

1. At low tide, look for animals that attach themselves to rocks. One of the oddest you might see are sea squirts. Depending on the kind, they look like blobs of jelly, hair or plastic. They may be as small as peas or as large as apples. On top, they have two earlike tubes or spouts. Water brings in food through one spout and waste water leaves through the other spout. If you touch a sea squirt GENTLY, it may squirt water.

2. Peer into cracks or holes in rocks for other animals, like snails and crabs. They like shady, moist spots.

3. Lift a few rocks at low tide. The sand or mud beneath them stays moist, so many kinds of animals may hide there. See what you can spot.

Wavy Water, Sandy Shores

Winds whip the surface of the sea into waves. Strong winds that travel for a long way across the sea make the biggest waves. When these waves hit the land, they strike with a lot of force, wearing some shores away.

In other places, waves build up the shores. Waves and wind throw sand onto a gentle slope—gradually making it wider. But the shore never stays the same. As long as there are winds and waves, the sand shifts constantly and new layers form.

Watch the Swash

1. Find swash marks on a sandy shore. They are thin, wavy lines made of fine ridges of sand, foam and bits of things from the sea, like broken shells or seaweed. Waves rush up the shore, then fall back, leaving swash marks that show how far the waves came. Follow these marks for a short distance. Then watch a new wave almost wash them away and leave its own swash marks on the shore.

2. Crawl along the wet side of swash marks and search for shallow domes of sand. The domes may be wider than your hand and deep enough to cover your fingernail. Waves make these domes by trapping air, which expands and lifts the sand. Poke a hole in one and watch it fall as the air inside escapes.

3. Hunt for special V-swash marks on the shore. When waves wash back over a stone or shell, they leave a mark that looks like the letter "V." See how many V-swash marks you can spot.

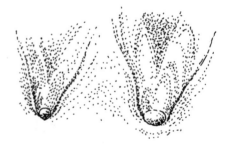

4. Now look for diamond-shaped marks on the shore. Check for a place where shallow waves wash back fast. Look for the diamond-shaped pattern they make across the sand.

Dig the Shore

1. Use your shovel or trowel to dig a hole in damp sand on a level part of the shore. Make the hole about the size of your pail.

2. On one side of the hole, check for small holes or gaps in the wall. Air that gets trapped in sand makes these openings.

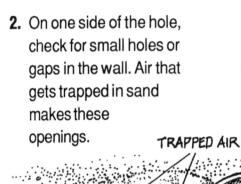

TRAPPED AIR

3. Smooth the wall of the hole with your shovel or trowel. Look for layers in the wall. On some shores, you will see few or no layers; on others, you may see several. Count them and write the number in your notebook. Compare this number with the number of layers you find at other shores.

4. Use your magnifying glass to look at the layers. They may be fine or coarse, light or dark, shiny or dull. They are clues about what has been happening in the sea. When the water is calm, for example, small shells may wash up and form chunky layers on a shore. When the water is stormy, waves may gather heavy minerals and make black layers on a shore.

5. Fill the hole with the sand you dug.

Wave Raves

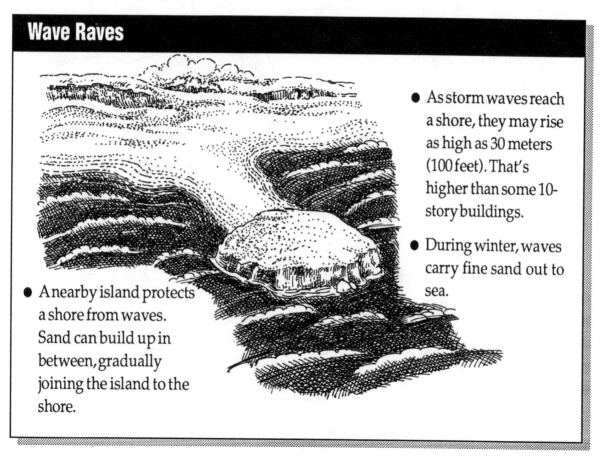

- A nearby island protects a shore from waves. Sand can build up in between, gradually joining the island to the shore.

- As storm waves reach a shore, they may rise as high as 30 meters (100 feet). That's higher than some 10-story buildings.

- During winter, waves carry fine sand out to sea.

Treasure Hunt

Treasure is much more than money, gold or jewels. Treasure is whatever people value. It may be something nature creates or something people make. It may be a living thing, an object, a feeling or a sound. It may be pretty, funny, rare or very old.

People often find treasure at the seashore. Some love the beautiful shells that waves wash up. In parts of the world, people have even used them for money.

Search for Shells

1. Walk high along the seashore to check what the waves have washed in. Along with seaweed and other things, there may be some empty shells.

2. Gather a few together. Notice the three layers in a shell: a thin outer layer that protects it, a thicker middle layer and a thin inner layer that is shiny and smooth. Feel the difference between the inside and the outside layers.

3. Hold the shells in bright sunlight. The thin layers of some kinds shine with many colors. On the outer layers, look for markings, like lines, speckles or spots. What an animal eats and the soil it lives in can affect the color and markings of its shells.

4. In your notebook, draw the shapes of shells you see. Each time you find a shell shaped like

one in your notebook, put a check beside the drawing. See which shape gets the most checks. Remember to leave the shells on the seashore.

Rattle Some Dollars

1. At low tide, look along a protected sandy shore for the flat, whitish skeleton of a sand dollar.

2. Notice how smooth it is. When it was alive, it was covered with little spines that helped it burrow into the seafloor or stand on edge to get bits of food in the water. After the sand dollar died, these spines fell off.

3. Look at the pattern on the top of the sand dollar—like a flower with five petals.

4. GENTLY shake the sand dollar close to your ear and listen for a rattle. That's the sound of the hard mouthparts rolling back and forth inside the skeleton.

Terrific Treasure

- Colored glass balls from Asian fishing nets sometimes break loose. Some float all the way across the Pacific Ocean and land—unbroken—on seashores in North America.

- There are about 70,000 kinds of shells in the world.

- Skeletons of some sand dollars have holes right through them. These holes help keep fast-flowing water from knocking down dollars standing on edge.

Hunt for Special Treasure

1. Read the list of objects, sounds or smells in "One Person's Seashore Treasure." See how many of them you can find—on this trip to the seashore, on the next and on the next. Use your notebook and pencil to write down what you find, but don't collect things. Leave them for the next treasure hunt.

2. Ask a friend to find the items in the list. Compare what you find with what your friend finds.

3. Make a list called "My Own Seashore Treasure." Find the items on it, then give the list to a friend.

One Person's Seashore Treasure

- Driftwood shaped like an animal
- Fresh, salty smell
- Feather with two colors in it
- Seaweed that feels like wet leather
- Loud sound from a non-living thing
- Green pebble with dark specks
- Cloud sailing in the wind
- Mass of sparkles
- Clear footprints in damp sand or mud
- Three sharp calls from the sky
- White-edged waves on the water
- Roughness and smoothness on the same thing
- Fine, wet spray
- Sunshine glinting off a silvery fish
- Something "riding" the wind

Index

Barnacles, 17, 45, 46, 54
Beach fleas, 53, 54
Beach hoppers, 53, 54
Birds, 30, 31, 34-38
Bladder wrack, 29
Bull kelp, 29

Chitons, 47
Clams, 14-17, 25, 39-42, 48, 49, 50
Cormorants, 37
Crabs, 22-26, 35, 43, 44, 46, 47,
   55

Decorator crabs, 25
Deep-sea clams, 42
Driftwood, 15, 16, 54, 63
Ducks, 36, 37

Fish, 8, 30-33, 35, 36, 37, 38, 43,
   44, 47, 63

Glass balls, 62
Goose barnacles, 17
Great blue herons, 31, 35, 37
Gribbles, 14-17
Gulls, 37, 38

Hermit crabs, 26
Herons, 31, 35, 37

Japanese spider crabs, 25

Kelp, 29

Limpets, 47
Lugworms, 52

Moon snails, 48-50
Mud, 10, 35, 38, 39, 40, 52, 55, 63
Muddy seashores, 10, 22, 52
Mussels, 45, 46

Oldsquaws, 37
Oyster thiefs, 29

Pea crabs, 25
Pebbles, 18, 19, 26, 63
Piddock clams, 42
Popping wrack, 29
Pop weed, 29

Razor clams, 42
Rock, 10, 18-21, 23, 27, 28, 31, 37,
   38, 43, 46, 47, 55
Rockweed, 29
Rocky shores, 10, 22, 23, 26, 28,
   32, 43, 44

Sailfish, 33
Sand, 10, 18, 20-21, 35, 39, 40, 49,
   50, 52, 54, 55, 56-59, 63
Sand dollars, 62
Sandhoppers, 53, 54
Sandy shores, 10, 18, 22, 48, 49,
   52, 56-59, 62
Sea anemones, 43, 45, 46
Sea lettuce, 28

Seascopes, 12, 13, 32, 44, 49
Sea squirts, 53, 55
Sea stars, 38, 43, 45, 46
Sea urchins, 45, 47
Seaweed, 8, 23, 25, 27-29, 35, 36,
   38, 44, 47, 54, 57, 61, 63
Shellfish, 36, 38, 46, 47 (see also
   clams and mussels)
Shells, 14, 22, 23, 24-25, 26, 29,
   38, 39, 40, 41, 42, 46, 48, 49,
   50, 54, 57, 59, 60, 61, 62
Shipworms, 14-17
Snails, 26, 48-50, 55
Spider crabs, 25
Sponges, 25, 46
Swash marks, 57

Tidepools, 8-9, 43-47
Tides, 9, 10, 15, 43
Treasure, 60-63

Waves, 9, 15, 18, 19, 21, 27, 51,
   54, 56-59, 60, 61, 63
Whale sharks, 33
Wood, 14, 15, 16, 54, 63
Wood borers, 14-17
Worms, 35, 47, 52